SHELTER

Margaret Hasse, poet

Sharon DeMark, artist

NODIN PRESS

Acknowledgments

The poem "House" revised from its first appearance as "Prairie Style" in the collection, *In a Sheep's Eye, Darling*, Milkweed Editions, appears with the permission of the author Margaret Hasse and the press. The poem "Canopy" excerpted from its first appearance as "With Trees" in the collection, *Between Us*, Nodin Press, appears with the permission of the author Margaret Hasse and the press.

The image for "Hideout" is based on a photograph by Jamie Grill used with the permission of Getty Images.

David Grothe, Joan Duffy Johnson, and Margaret Todd Maitland provided valuable response to the manuscript.

Library of Congress Control Number: 2020944604

ISBN: 978-1-947237-31-5

Nodin Press
5114 Cedar Lake Road
Minneapolis, MN 55416

Printed in USA

For the people, places, and things
that give us all shelter

Contents

Introduction

Poet Margaret Hasse and artist Sharon DeMark have been colleagues in Minnesota's arts education field, practicing artists, and friends over several decades. Soon after the Covid-19 virus became a major threat in the United States in March 2020, residents in our state and across the country began sequestering at home or in whatever places they could find.

Feeling the isolation of social distancing and the increasing vulnerability of our community, Margaret reached out in an e-mail to see if Sharon would be interested in a collaborative project responding to the current time. Sharon enthusiastically agreed to a partnership that would allow us to inspire one another's creativity while being physically sequestered. We began to plan what to do together.

Because of the pandemic, the universal human need for protection and safety was on our minds. We took shelter—broadly defined or imagined in real terms or metaphorically—as the subject of our endeavor. The arrangement we conceived had each of us initiating either a poem (Margaret) or an artwork (Sharon) about a safe haven of her choice to which the other would respond, often with a new vision of the subject.

After creating a number of pieces, we realized that a collection was forming that might be meaningful to others. A book—which is a type of refuge—became the means to share our work. Over four months we completed thirty coupled words and images about a variety of places and experiences. Some of the shelters serve urgent needs, such as a hospital and a sanctuary for immigrants. Some are whimsical (hug) or for animals (barn). Others, such as canopy, cave and snow, reflect the way we both see the natural world as a harboring force.

Margaret's poetry in this book includes lyrics, narratives, list poems, prose poems and one each of these forms: concrete, haibun, persona, riddle, and patterned rhyme. Sharon's paintings are watercolors; most are on cold press 140-pound paper in sizes ranging from 5½" x 7½" to 11" x 15". The poem or painting that sparked each collaboration appears on the left-hand page of *Shelter*.

We hope that readers will be delighted and comforted by the protective places depicted here that sustain life.

– Margaret Hasse and Sharon DeMark

It is in the shelter of each other that the people live.

—   Irish proverb

The ache for home lives in all of us, the safe place where we can go as we are and not be questioned.

—   Maya Angelou

Whether we are under an umbrella on a sidewalk wrapped in complicity and conversation, or alone immersed in the pages of a good book, we're happily held in our private sphere but still conscious of the shape of our sanctuary.

—   Louisa Thomsen Brits

ART

As the sun begins to build its house of gold
an artist is called to her window.
Alone in the attic of creation
free to leave her body, lift bird-like
and settle on bare branches,
she can portray what is before,
within or beyond herself.
With pencil, paper, color,
she paints an upside-down bowl
of blue essence some call heaven.
Anne Frank, too, in the bolt-hole
of a tiny annex found her patch
of sky and shared her vision.
She wrote in her diary: *Think
of all the beauty in yourself and
everything around you and be happy.*

BARN

The barn like an ark
rode waves of prairie grass,
anchored in cornfields.
Dairy cows lumbered
into the building's dusk.
Skittish cats came near to lick
milk squirted at their sharp faces.
In the doorway white chickens
pecked and dusted.
Maybe a pony in its stall, pigs in a pen...
Maybe a boy in the hot loft
stacking bales of alfalfa and dry straw
bound with hairy twine.

When humans and their livestock
left, the abandoned barn
welcomed wild animals.
A pair of foxes took up
residence under the roof.
Vegetation thick around
the foundation harbored
rabbits and quail.
Lizards dozed on cool concrete.
Swallows colonized the eaves
with mud-pellet nests
darting and turning in flight
under the long gaze of light.

BELLY

Hey little astronaut
        floating in the fluid
of inner space
        attached to the mothership
by a cord, cosseted
        and coveted, you
                human-to-be

within your protected
        red universe
           of heat
             and heartbeat

come, we're eager to see
        your face when you complete
            your marvelous mission
and are equipped
        to live here on Earth.

BIVOUAC

In the dream he's once again
a boy in the forest
encircled by tall trees
alone to fend for himself,
forage for kindling, start
a fire, unpack his survival kit,
prepare for the night
by building a cone-shaped
shelter with long tree limbs.
Tips of evergreen branches
and dry leaves make a bed.
All his life he'll love the smell
of crushed pine needles.
As he falls asleep he remembers
to thank the trees.

BOOK

Remember those Saturdays you read stories when it rained?
The night you stayed up late to finish a book
about a horse that made you cry at the end?
Remember picture books
that included boys and girls that looked like you,
the book you read with a flashlight in a tent,
its mesh vents open to the stars?
You became open to the stars.
Remember the heavy book wrapped in plastic
and carried to school in a snow storm,
the book boarded like a boat to a surprise party,
the one claimed from the cove of a Little Free Library,
the one you didn't know you needed until you received the gift?
And the poetry book where each poem
was like fragrance of a new flower?
Later you found out about Mars' mysteries
and the way to plant potatoes.
You learned words like potpourri and weltschmerz.
You traveled to places like the Bight of Biafra
and Renaissance England, hearing voices, many voices.
You loved a book you wore ragged and bought another copy
to fill with margin notes.
You keep returning to that small tan book
where you found your soul.

BUS SHELTER

Although it's ten degrees
below zero, overhead
a metal palm tree
topped by snow
arcs the benches.
When my bus arrives
on its regular route
conveying no other
passengers, I board
and blurt out to
the impetuous brown
in the driver's eyes:
Let's get away from this!

*I always hated
cold*, the driver
says and turns
renegade, driving
us far off route.
That night in a warmer
place we stop,
step out on a side road
beneath an endless
rosary of stars
before heading on
to Arizona, Mexico,
and all points south.

*– Artist Marcia McEachron created tropical public art for a
bus stop at the corner of Fairview and University Avenues,
St. Paul, Minnesota.*

CANOPY

Like a child I sit down, lie back,
look up at the crowns of maple,
needled spruce, and a big-hearted boxwood.

Fugitive birds dart in and out.
In the least little wind, birch leaves turn
and flash silver like a school of minnows.

Clouds range in the broad sky
above Earth's great geniuses
of shelter and shade.

CAR

Comfortable—
In his 1938 black Cadillac, a grandfather drives through Forest Park,
his two granddaughters in the backseat
tucked with lap robes on both sides of a willow-gray armrest.

Free—
Mother of five kids takes a spin alone in her 1956 Ford Fairlane
around the block to smoke her one cigarette of the day.

Private—
Away from fuddy-duddy parents, two teens neck in a 1968 Chevy
Impala as the radio plays the Monkees' *You May Just Be the One.*

Self-sufficient—
1974 VW Camper. Orange. The couple has everything
within reach: new scenery, food, clothes, books, bed, one another.

Safety Net—
A man who's lost his job and almost all else lives out
of his rusted and dented 1986 Toyota Corolla, clothes in the trunk.

Cozy—
A parent at the wheel of a 1995 Buick Roadmaster station wagon
heads home through the dark with a child dozing to the whir of tires,
huff of heater, and tiny lights of the dashboard merging with stars.

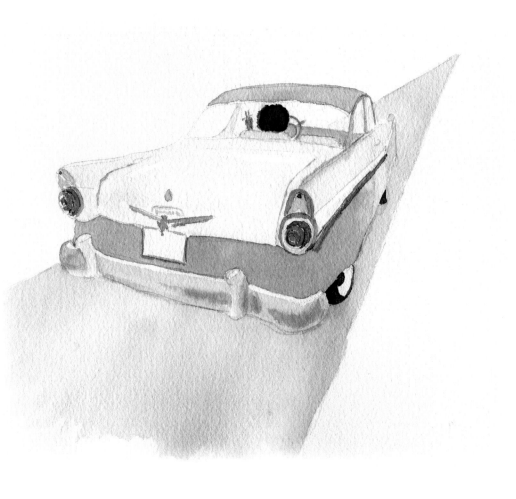

CAVE

A tawny swirl of sandstone
carved by wind and water
offers a chamber for us
to sit out the storm.

It seems we're not alone.
Spray-painted graffiti put
Tom plus Joan here in a heart.
Others also left their markings.

Through centuries caves
have been retreats for hermits,
jails, burial vaults, places
to make cheese—or to dance.

Cro-Magnon people conjured
a good hunt using colors
carried in hollow bones
to draw fat deer on the walls.

We wait quietly in this golden
room, marking only time
until skies clear and it's safe
to leave the cave's embrace.

CHUPPAH

Your first home was the cocoon
in your mother.
Then you were held
in the anchorage of arms,
all hungers allayed.

You played house
in long grass or under sheets
draped over tables.

Once you camped out
in a tent, that temporary lodging
that leaked in the night.

Later you dwelled in a dorm room
then an apartment's
honeycombed housing
where you shared walls
with neighbors and heard them
dance on the floor above.

When you loved, your beloved
became haven.

When you married
you two stood under a canopy
open on all sides.

In the future home
of your togetherness
you welcome all guests
whether known or strangers
including a new child.

CLOTHING

Clothes press against
the glass window
of a washing machine
like faces in the rain.
After they've spun
in the big dryer, I fold
my baby's plush onesies,
my son's favorite jeans,
and T-shirts my husband
taught me to roll
like window shades
when it's my turn
to do the laundry.
I stack up the items
then hug everything
to my chest, smelling
warm clean cotton
that covers the ones I love.

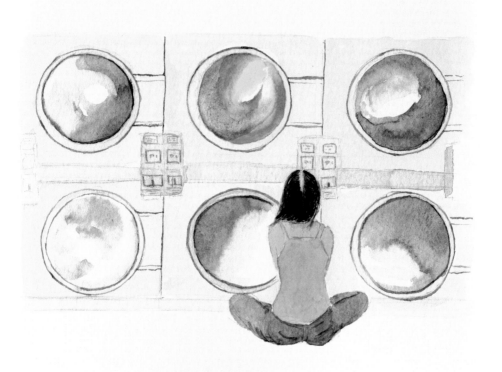

HIDEOUT

It's too quiet in the house.
WHERE DID THE BOYS GO?
We walk with heavy feet
and talk in capital-letter voices.
WHAT ARE THOSE BOXES DOING THERE?
WE'LL HAVE TO THROW THEM AWAY!
We pretend we don't hear giggles
like steam escaping a radiator.
We call out the window
PLEASE COME HOME,
then hear a rustle like dry leaves
in the corner of the room.
NOW WE WILL HAVE TO EAT
THE COOKIES ALL BY OURSELVES.
Not cats, not Styrofoam popcorn,
not Jack-in-the-Boxes,
but two boys pop up grinning.
We proclaim their appearance
an act of magic, and after
the hiding and the finding,
everyone orders milk with
their cookies.

HOSPITAL

In marble temples of Greece, priests
of Asclepius—a doctor and a demi-god—
assessed complaints of pilgrims and interpreted
their dreams. Wormwood was prescribed
for a woman with a gut ache, the licking tongue
of a sacred dog for a man's gashed hand.

In 2020 when I check into a hospital, I turn
my body over to a doctor with a kind face
and years of education. I get the care
required to heal: procedures, medication
through an IV, and nourishment on a tray
delivered to my clean bed.

Near midnight on rubber-soled shoes a nurse
with steady hands steals into my room to check
my vital signs. *Are you hot? Are you breathing?*
In my muzzy state, I pull snug the blanket
of deeper slumber. Like the ancient Greeks
I'm dreaming a miraculous cure.

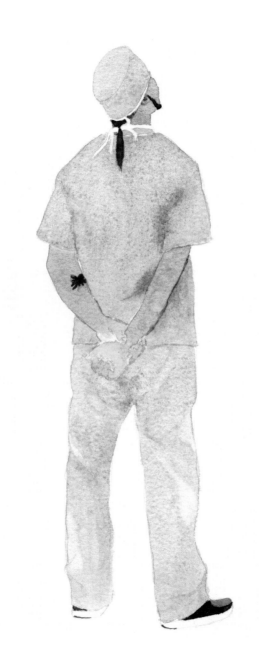

HOUSE

Sometimes I walk by a house so perfect
I want to buy it and stay forever if I could.
But someone already lives here. A woman
shy as a new moon peeks from the back
garden wearing a flowered hat. I turn away.
Such regret: I have only one body to live in.
I stand across the street to look. The building
reveals itself slowly like a face I've decided to love.
The windows open out. How I'd like to be the one
to push the cranks in their miniature orbits opening
the windows for the evening tatters of cool air.
In the stucco house the color of burnt sienna
I'd wear a kimono, feast on orange juice
and apples, and be totally happy in a way
we're never really happy except for a moment,
except for right now.

HUG

To fit together
is one branch
in the language
root of "arm."
How regrettable
that arms name
hardware of war.
The only right
to bear arms safely
is the caring capacity
of our amazing
appendages that
comfort and caress,
have and hold,
cradle and rock,
clasping each other
close.

HUT

Hikers with backpacks
trudge along switchbacks.
The trail etched on
mountainsides is often
wet and snow-packed.
With endurance and luck
they arrive at the bare shoulder
of Gunsight Pass.

Beside the plummet of gorge
between juts of sleek peaks
above a glacial blue lake,
icy cold in summer,
a stone hut stands spartan
as a bone where visitors
find respite on their passage
through the wild.

   – *This hut, built in 1932, stands on Gunsight Pass,*
     elevation 6,946 feet, Glacier National Park.

MOUSE HOUSE

To most mice
a pile of brush in the woods
or a dark corner of a garage is home.

But to one mouse
has been given a minute wooden A-frame
with a portico roof over the entrance.

After Stuart Little drove north out
of the pages of E. B. White's book,
perhaps he found his friend Margolo

in Minnesota and retired here
in this wonder of the mouse real estate world
situated on prime property in Hidden Falls

near a stream that slips by like a dream.

    – *The sign on this "Mouse Sanctuary" in an urban
     park requests, "Please leave alone, or offer a snack!"*

NEIGHBORHOOD

May a neighbor spare a cup of rice.
May a neighbor stoop down to learn
a child's name—*It's Wesley, is it?*
May a neighbor watch the house
of another who's gone.
May neighbors shovel an extra length
of sidewalk when someone is ill.
May they avoid prying questions.
May they be neighborly,
not judge each other for being
introverted or extroverted
and be not clannish but accept
their Boo Radleys and Mr. Rogers,
their Yangs and their Ahmeds.
A wave of a neighbor's hand
like the spring wind
signifies warmth and welcome.

NEST

That slim year we found the nest
newly vacant. We'd watched
two blue eggs become chicks now

grown and gone toward their own lives
as our son had just fledged and flown.
And the nest—a brown bowl within

white veils of flowering bushes—
still sturdy after the robins left.
It was made of twigs and mud,

lined with dry grasses, and strands
of dark hair from an outdoor haircut
that left our son's wild nimbus

short as he wanted for his departure.
Migratory birds often return.
We held on to that.

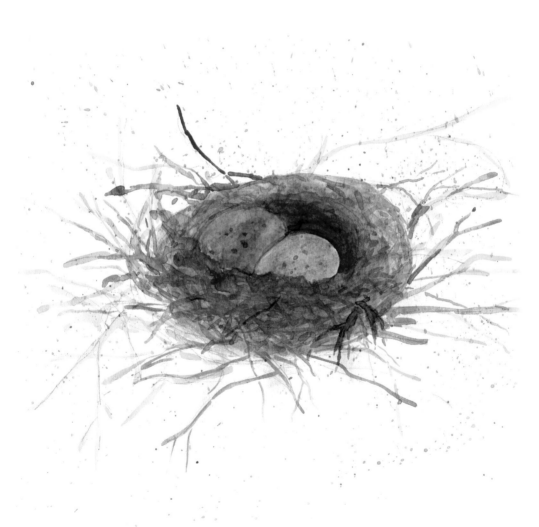

PATHWAY

Trust a route that
people and animals make.
Many have walked here
where plants dwindle
to bare ground.
Whether it's slim or wide,
sandy or earthen,
brick, pebbled, or plain,
choose a footpath through
the remote or the tame.
Avoid slashing
brush and bramble.
Let a path take you
somewhere gently, perhaps
to a new view of things.
A silver river in the valley
is also on its way.

PLAYHOUSE

On the lawn across the street
a new playhouse stands
like a homestead shanty
in the shadow of its parent house
for the girl whose mother
just back from the hospital
nurses a new baby sister.

The girl carries an armload
of dolls to her small building
and sits them all in a circle
as if at a garden party
where she feeds each one
a plate of grass
and a little cup of dew.

PORCH

Even this hot summer it happens
the porch has its Saturday mornings
of ease, its trees and bird song through the leaves.
We drag chairs to the open air,
settle in to watch the walkers parade by
on city sidewalks with ears pressed
to the seashells of their small phones.
Sometimes we call out to a friend or wave
to the red-haired toddler in a stroller waving at us.

Even in this heat everyone else seems intent
on important business ahead.
The dogs pull on their leashes and girls jog past
leaving a trail of glittering laughter.

We're at the age we don't mind
being passed by; ambition has left us calm
and easy in our wicker chairs, books in our laps.
We just want to linger on the porch
as if on vacation, observing people
and scenery part of and apart from us.
The porch with its deck and white balustrades
carries us like a boat on smooth water
toward the long afternoon.

SANCTUARY CHURCH

We came here in the rain. I brought my doll.
The room is little and clean. Sometimes
there is singing of many people in the walls.
Shh, Mama touches fingers to my lips. It's secret
how we got to this place.

We used to live by Grandmother. My school
had a red door. We slept on the floor
when guns shot. The coo of pigeons came in the light.

We hide because we have no papers.
The women with food bring papers for me
to draw on and crayons bright as gold.
My mother says that the women
have hearts of gold I cannot see.

Someday we will leave for a house with no fear.
It will be good like eating when you are hungry.
And this is how we live. And this is how we live.

    – After Randall Jarrell's "Protocols"

SHELL

To the red fox, its lair dug in the earth.
To the common rabbit, a warren.
To the ant, its concealed colony
beneath a dirt mound.
A bee has its hive.
A burrow for the ground squirrel
and a lodge for the beaver.
Mud to the frog.
To the coyote, its den.
To the Arctic polar bear, its ice cave
and to the woodpecker, a cavity in a tree.
Weed tangles provide cover for fish.
The whitetail deer beds on the ground
between timber and marsh.
The turtle in its shell carries its security
from egg to its watery world.

SNOW

Why not call snow a haven?
Here on flat and open fields
seedlings of wheat wait winterlong
under a wide white cover.

Wet loam black as a raven
emerges, then earth yields
shimmering green and birdsong
just after spring melt is over.

STORM CELLAR

Dark clouds on the horizon. Father stares southwest as if reading
the news. High heat. Stillness. When a siren wails from town,
quick Mother gathers lunch from the picnic table in her
Fourth of July tablecloth. Children with flashlights
are herded through a door in the earth and
down stairs to a dank room festooned by
cobwebs. Backs against cool concrete,
we eat, play card games, listen for a
twister's rumble with its spinning
vortex of cars and fruit trees,
chickens, bicycles and barn
doors. Silence lengthens
like a long shadow.
An air horn blasts
three times
all clear.

We emerge into unharmed lives
blinking like nocturnal animals in dazzling light.

TENEMENT

As tourists we're shepherded down a warren of dim hallways, peer into open doors. History, in the voice of Tatianna, our tour guide, adopts a brisk tone: *By 1900 some 2.3 million immigrants were living in tenement housing like this in New York City. A family of 10 might occupy 325 square feet of space.* We try to picture where they put their clothes. How could they sleep, laid out like logs on the floor? We think of our closets, our palatial mattresses. Tatianna continues: *No running water. One outhouse for 20 residents.* Someone's distant cousin Bridget fled the Great Hunger. Uncle Max left pogroms in Russia and four family graves. They are among those who found their first residence in a big new country over-crowded, thin-walled, unvented. We stare into tight rooms that housed so many lives, see signs of punishing poverty, but also aspiration and domestic care in daisies embroidered on the tablecloth, a book marked with a ribbon, the chipped blue pitcher for fetching water.

    – *The Tenement Museum, located in the Lower East Side*
      of Manhattan, New York City, is a National Historic Site.

TENT

It was difficult to see her, the thin girl in a parka
protecting her cardboard sign from snowflakes
drifting up like insects in the wind
as you drove home from Target in a car humming
with heat and music.

Her refuge, a riffraff of fabric and plastic sheets,
draped over a broken shopping cart like a tent for ghosts.
Her back was up against the wall, the cart, the cold,
the dark and those of us who passed by
without noticing.

UMBRELLA

Clues to a riddle in eight lines:

When carried in the past, a symbol of prestige.
What can be sturdy as a long bone?
What's not usually a fair-weather friend?
What is often left behind, forgotten?

Without one, a face might be washed.
What succumbs to forces that turn it inside out?
What decorates a beach and bans a burn?
What tents two lovers who kiss?

VIVARIUM

The image of a Mason jar sparks memories of my mother putting
up raspberry preserves. In grade school, my summer lips ripe red
from sampling, I caught fireflies in a jar with air-holes hammered
into the top with a nail. The busy blinking lights by my bedside
made me think I'd grasped a star cluster to release in the morning.
What type of plant does the jar in the painting hold? In third
grade we each brought a sweet potato to school, stuck toothpicks
into its sides, hung it from the rim of a glass of water so most was
submerged. Our teacher wanted her students to nurture something
green, learn what it needed—fresh water, warmth, sunshine. Roots
pale as rice noodles grew. Vines sprouted from the top. Could the
plant in this jar be like the one WALL-E preserved to restart our
ruined world? In 1960 a man sealed a plant in a large glass bottle to
create a protected eco-system still thriving today.

The plant in glass is
like Earth enfolded in its
fragile atmosphere.

About the Poet and Artist

Margaret Hasse has authored five collections of poems, most recently *Between Us,* winner of the Midwest Poetry Prize. She co-edited *Rocked by the Waters: Poems of Motherhood* (2020). Margaret has received poetry fellowships or grants from the National Endowment for the Arts, Minnesota State Arts Board, and The Loft-McKnight. As a teaching poet, she's helped diverse people write and read poetry in prisons, community centers, nonprofit organizations, and schools. Margaret has also been involved with the community as an arts consultant.

Sharon DeMark celebrated 2019 by committing to painting a daily watercolor. During the year she presented two exhibits. Proceeds from the sale of her paintings supported several Minnesota nonprofits. Sharon's artwork has been published in two editions of the *Saint Paul Almanac* and one of her paintings was selected for the *Almanac's* "Poetry in the Park in the Dark" partnership with Frogtown Farm. She has worked for theaters and performing arts centers helping to connect youth, educators, and artists. Sharon currently works in philanthropy.